T0154507

BLUE *STRANGER*

WITH

MOSAIC BACKGROUND

WAYNE

KOESTENBAUM *BLUE*

STRANGER WITH

MOSAIC BACKGROUND

TURTLE POINT **PRESS**

NEW YORK 2012

Published by Turtle Point Press
www.turtlepointpress.com
Copyright © 2012 by Wayne Koestenbaum
All rights reserved
ISBN 978-1-933527-60-4
LCCN 2011930738
Printed on acid-free, recycled paper
in the United States of America

|

||

FOR STEVEN MARCHETTI

INVESTIGATION

I might benefit from supplemental testosterone.
My arm is missing a wedge.

My girlfriend had a much-touted abortion.
I'm not emotionally expressive.

Adorno: "He who offers for sale
something unique that no one wants to buy

represents, even against his will,
freedom from exchange."

I sucked off two bastards.
My lamé purse announces social class.

I use fado as template.
My tattoo is fading.

I asphyxiated Hölderlin in his tower.
Like Fassbinder, I died at 37.

Like nature, I am in heat.
I forgot my diegetic name.

I am John Lennon's lover.
I abhor anachronism.

4

POSSESSIVENESS

the atonality of folded underwear

the Tel Aviv of Chinese water torture

the Martians of *My Three Sons*

the parsimony of Tel Quel

the archivist of beatitudes

the Helsinki of Frankenstein

the Winchester Mystery House of devil-may-care

the worldwide franchise of Croatian mystery plays

the Bettie Page of situationism

the New Criticism of Ethel Waters

the marble pound cake of tauromachy

the *Christopher Strong* of *Sesame Street*

the Michèle Morgan of abstinence

the 19 Berggasse of Calvin Klein

the stifling corridor of condom leakage

the Boris Karloff of Maiden Lane

the CalArts of maple syrup

the Lord's Prayer of Rumpelstiltskin

the Gretchen's Spinning Song of fatuous praise

the Eli Wallach of pragmatism

the meal ticket of the Williamsburg Messiah

the Mrs. Robinson of Abstract Expressionism

the mead-soaked sheets of Melanctha

the Abbott and Costello of ostinato

the abracadabra of panty-hose

the *Guys and Dolls* of pineapple upside-down cake

the Hungry I of Shangri-La

the Bog Man of Capitol Hill

the Beresford of bilge

RETURN OF THE NOUN

Behold the library bombed, the ancient scrolls defaced,
    the Warsaw Concerto decomposed in delirium,

every salmonella scare a screen memory,
    carcasses and Erinyes a mob of questionables,

The Sorcerer's Apprentice a slashed *Metamorphosen,*
    The Birds no more vital than polio vaccines,

the Rubens drawing and the Pee-wee Herman lawsuit two
    motes in God's eye,
    his brain on fire with Ali Baba's nothingness,

compartmentalizations collapsed like a Vatican tchotchke,
    Retin-A interchangeable with Rastafarian fantasy,

mucus membranes and Trojans available through the mail,
    Proust too in need of Sani-Wipes,

a dot on the nose no more lethal than a dot on the moon,
  Stokowski angry, Garbo in retreat,

vegan hallucinogens in the adolescent bedroom,
  the bedwetter and Anna Freud equally up in arms,

she who stands and waits and she who conks out,
  Aufhebung and *Clavierübung* friends at last,

crematoria and minimalists,
  onion rings on the side,

the circumcision botched and John Money dead,
  the hot dog bun well-buttered,

the fistula and the ticker-tape parade,
  the soul a falafel sandwich for $3.99,

the obviousness of CorningWare and the Nannerl Mozart
  orgone box,
    the return of the noun in her figure-fitting automobile,

the logician's karma in the catacombs,
    opium sauce over Thoreau

when the sphincter starts behaving like a treatise,
    the striking Philharmonic unable to recant,

the potty under erasure, Leslie Caron *meshuggana,*
    Hindemith becoming Liza and Judy at the mildew Palace,

the straight man's Adorno mustachioed and curlicued,
    the eyewitness and the dialectician, the teak and the
    cordovan,

the pedophile and the pediatrician, the porcelain and the
    lunar,
    the article slashed, the culpable comma

borne on a tide of adjacent Bel Air mansions
    here with Lorna Luft and other Luddites,

a perforated performance the *verklempt* daisies have
assembled for you
in time for final editing and dissemination

AT THE GRAVE OF

FERNANDO PESSOA

Pessoa's basement toilet didn't flush.
Dream: my toy gun shot a vegan.

■

I saw the queen of Portugal's bidet
and ate wiggly custard cups at Pessoa's café.

■

My motto: "Have ChapStick, Will Travel."
Dream: an oft-married adventuress owned a house four
    miles long.

■

A teenaged boy muff-dived on a secluded stair
near flaming William Beckford's Monserrate.

■

My biceps have a duck's gelatinousness: elliptical
eroticism. Octopus salad. Four dried figs.

■

At dinner I asked, "What makes Gandhi tick?"
Flea market, Tomar: I saw a man peeing.

■

From afar, his penis appeared purple,
patterned. Perhaps it was his shirt cuff?

■

Two taciturn elders brooded on a synagogue stoop.
Molding their faces, God quit midstream.

■

Jaw spasms of an old man guarding a dead end:
confronting his aggrieved dyskinesia, my car U-turned.

■

Dreamt I didn't give my phone number
to Paul Newman, although he'd asked.

■

Joanne Woodward snubbed me until I shouted,
"Let's blow up our idiosyncracies!"

■

"To write, for me, is to despise myself,"
Pessoa said, "but I can't stop writing."

■

Near the gilded Tagus, a toothless lady
twice held up a beggar's cup. I twice refused.

17

FAUST'S DOG

Inflexible, I can't auto-fellate.
I'd love to meet a self-sucker, photograph him.

■

Circularity, serpentine, labyrinth:
all three words apply.

■

Stacked records fall on the platter
to produce—with a hitch—posthumous quartets.

■

Each time I use the word *poignant*
I discover it contains puncture.

■

Heritage is a Kim Novak word—
her Polish past, surpressed in *Picnic.*

■

Hecuba's tears, my mother said,
appear in *The Iliad.*

■

My turncoat behavior
transformed her to teak or cork.

■

Every action, hillside, and flower
rewards investigation.

■

Assignment: see every film featuring Ernest Borgnine
and then write a 500-word essay about his career.

■

Assignment: stay at a motel in a town without attractions.
Choose your town carefully—make sure it has no attractions.

■

Dream: Tom Cruise, sitting on my lap,
said my shirt smelled like skunk or neglect.

■

My right thumb has a scar
shaped like an empty skiff too minuscule for pity.

■

The bird outside my window might return,
attracted by the smell of boiling potatoes.

■

Forgive men's hairy upper arms,
cabinets displaying accomplishment or decrepitude.

■

My butt, at its best, resembles Faust's dog.
It has an affectionate relationship to condiments.

■

Gounod's *Faust* doesn't omit infanticide.

My Achilles heel: overstatement.

■

Dream: a baby in an overheated car told me,
"I'm not positive, sir, but my diaper might contain two dark
  elements."

POEM ON PINK

CONSTRUCTION PAPER

Write ten syllables about a landscape.
Pink leaves veil crude neighbors. Sap's a kilim.

■

I crossed a barbed wire fence to McDonald's
and distributed anti-slaughterhouse propaganda.

■

The heavy cream went bad. I read aloud
a Lacan line about the stupid signifier.

■

The psychologist judged my dick a "perky" affair.
In the future we might add Calvados to the apple crisp.

■

German makes clear distinctions between active and passive,
standing and being commanded to stand.

■

Beachcombers ambled through the auto-hypnotic crêche
in our backyard banyan tree's shade.

■

Coleridge, despite bad digestion, coined the words
"bisexual," "psycho-somatic," and "immanence."

■

Julia Child told me not to make fun of her mother
although Julia's house was a make-fun-of-Mom terrarium.

■

After Obama was elected president
I dreamed I climbed steep stairs.

■

Before departure I plucked the last green pole beans.
When the bean plant decides to stop producing, it simply stops.

HOT SCENES WITH

UNDEAD HEMATOLOGISTS

The hematologist says, "Unbutton your trousers."
His complexion resembles Boris Karloff's.

■

I fingerfuck a poet.
He turns into a novelist.

■

And yet, like a cheroot,
he functions as father.

■

A smoke column rises from the Bauhaus.
Hot and cold colors interact.

■

Beethoven is no antidote,
not even the incompetently played *Pastoral*.

■

One bee per veronica stem.
One bee per speedwell.

■

Selva oscura of pubes is ideal.
Keep privates murky.

■

My father reaches out toward sea wind
or is himself sea wind.

■

He chops a sponge into pieces,
throws them in the soup, and lowers the flame to nearly zero.

■

I tell my hematologist,
"We need to discuss scabs, hyperventilation . . ."

■

I lose easy gravity.
I contract gravid ease.

ACCRETION

The window's wooden edge creates
snotty boxes, accidentally.

■

I blew him, he blew me:
ordinary linguistic event.

■

Glimmers gang up:
primitive accretion.

■

Recall the lumpy father's mourning tux
near gay lib's farmhouse.

■

Recall the lumpy mother's overt wiggle,
her "Für Elise" delusion on velvet.

■

She commutes in a Fonda-like Honda.
My speech grows stumbly, lardy.

■

I stash four kids
in the clothes dryer. The least

■

duplicitous kid's
fur fills the lint drawer with business.

SATURNALIA

God is a ski bunny.
I must make clear my sexual availability.

■

In modern art we need more gelding, more fringe.
Dimples are gessoed into place by random particles—
"if" and "be."

■

Vista of evisceration: Susan Hayward near a fine flamenco
college.
Which toilet will I use in Peter Handke's summerhouse?

■

I ate the wrong baloney.
Prognosis: lifelong acne in a greige smock.

■

Defensively the baby reverts to curd size.
Its hobby is saying "vroom."

CRAWL SPACES

I crawled backward to Mexico
through an Egyptian or Czech window
uphill with a pimply bar-girl and her shyster husband.

■

Guilty, young, expectorating,
she ate home-grown cumquats.
Don't borrow her bounty—grow your own cumquats.

■

Not each of these categories is equal.
Consider Eichmann's trial
and Donny Osmond, their noncongruence.

■

Dark and drecky in Athens today
in Dublin.
Miserly clumps of brake.

GOOD MORNING, MARIENBAD

My lime-green pantsuit rebuked
hostile art boys running,
in bras, across a tract house rumpus room.

■

I cut a tiny quadrant off my face
and drowned the excerpt
in a rock cleft's rivulet.

■

Off-topic lisp in the frigidarium:
I bit the wolfman's wombat ass.
No more fake Delmore Schwartz gestures!

■

With "lyric" and "Wittgenstein"
tattooed on his revolutionary belly
he smelled of a frilly biochemical process for nearly thirty
    minutes.

31

■

Michael Jackson (whose red breast
hangs down) stole
limelight from the Keystone Kops said a transitional god.

POINTILLISM

I bumped into Sinatra's bone
during mother's Rasputin
phase: lackadaisical interlude.

■

"Dah-cweem":
baby-talk ice cream.
Permit him a growth spurt.

■

Radical faeries offer
forced sterilization
to newts and toads.

■

Spillane is diffident.
Are houris synchronized?
Vamoose, soliloquy.

∎

If the urethra is his or hers
the pet monkey effect applies:
fallacy of the monad.

∎

Gonad? Now I can't
remember the hideously
logical Lydian conception.

∎

Inarticulateness begets
this whack-off area,
Super Bowl audible.

∎

I regress. Circe
is a misty integument.
Browse these cracks.

■

Colt, Titan, *doxa,*
Ritalin, Elliott Gould,
Saks, Farsi, *pharmakon.*

■

I regress. Wigglers,
unite! Happy
are we to be nothing.

THE NEW BRUTALISM

This exercise demands
the largest possible
conceptual frame.

"You're hot."
"No, *you're* hot."
Only one of them is hot.

■

Eyebrows feral,
Patrick sucks my toes.
(I worm his name out of him.)

His dugs are tax
write-offs. He offers
instant contamination.

■

Let's bogart a cup of joe.
I recognize you
from the talent show.

You were wearing
the best chocolate
floor-length number.

■

The jock's crack
is unsentimental, zitty.
Clean it with a clammy cloth.

Its composure keeps
flatted thirds
at bay, occults activism.

■

Minimalism:
I like to wear
v-necked t-shirts.

The difference
between v and t
is minimal.

■

Clock heard through leaves.
Spittoon overflowing. The shy
shrimpy girl across the street

wants me to rim her husband—
a desire she communicates
through magic-marker murals.

THE TIDBIT SCHOOL OF

ADULT ENTERTAINMENT

My favorite TV program
is *Green Acres*.
It has everything I need:

breeze, breast augmentation,
vocabulary, dry cleaning,
Miracle-Gro, positivism.

■

The palace hallways are diseased.
A tube of Tinkertoys
poses as penicillin.

Salome waits near the fire screen.
She wants to tinkle:
not permitted.

■

Whoa! I tell
my father awful things.
As a result, the future

is sick. Two *Trovatore* arias
become hyper-realistic,
dystopian. One spits upon the other.

■

My brother discovers the horse farm.
I have second fiddle status.
And I'm not even a fiddle.

Four stoats race around my body—
or am I pursuing them?
I'm not even a third fiddle, or a fourth.

■

Sorbet. Primal ooze.

My father erases our last name.

Swinging in summer sun

I'm driven to repeat

the library smell of waiting

for alphabetization to arise.

■

Giddy-up giddy-up.

Expressivity is dead.

So is Red Buttons.

I don't want to read

about Lebanon or Israel.

That stance backfires.

GROOMING IN AMERICA

Jackie O volunteers as docent,
a decrepit museum—
New Orleans? I line up.

■

Time to buy a christening gift.
Tricia Nixon speaks Catalan
and takes cuts. *Tempus fugit.*

■

Cast of thousands: nude husbands
soak in redwood hot-tubs
to celebrate daughterly loyalty.

■

Qualified linguists confirm:
my grooming skills are peerless.
The soccer coach's concentration

precludes small talk.
Inclusion serves as a caress:
after the rooster crows,

a father—leg hair abraded
by years of tube socks—
includes me in his categories.

NEBBISH ARCHIVE

You look like Burt Lancaster
in *Kiss the Blood Off My Hands.*
Palladio's Teatro Olimpico
achieves a similar, baffling detachment.

∎

Father and mother watch the attractive boy
masturbate for pay.
His wallflower has stamina.
Upside down it resembles Rumpelstiltskin.

∎

Mortality makes lush orchestration obsolete.
Tokyo Drifter features torch singers
whose makeup is Anna Moffo's in 1967:
pancake as propitiation.

∎

44

The President is a castrated dreamer
with a tonsure. Liz interviews him on TV,
displays condescension, plays dulcimer,
condenses her questions into four blots.

LITTLE ODE TO INCORRIGIBILITY

Boy with snot running out his nose,
a disease, head down,
no one knows what to do with him,
he lives near paradise.

■

He steals my clown pants,
piecemeal, through hatchets and flattery.
I worship his requirements in a sex cave.
My mother's toiletries stand sentinel.

■

Grab incorrigibility.
Electrocute or garotte it.
Incorrigibility originates dance?
Say something offensive involving rivers.

URINALS

AFTER MIKE BIDLO'S "FOUNTAIN DRAWINGS"

The urinal was trained
to be straightforward.

Its judicial manner,
a cistern, grows more adequate each minute.

■

The urinal leans to the right
like a druid from *The Seventh Seal.*

Its fur cap
is a Goldie Hawn of immanence.

■

47

The urinal hangs over the antediluvian
planet's edge. Hasty

is the snow of the urinal's
Legion of Honor smile.

■

The urinal hosts a mouse
whose tail curls repeatedly

as if the first time it curled
someone was asking to be saved from the second time it curled.

■

With its polyphony of spanking and calculus,
the urinal makes Palestrina jealous.

It wants to be more
than a semi-colon in the hospital.

■

The urinal's buttocks, labia
reincarnated, sit

on their triumvirate throne, three Elizabeths,
no longer a blank habitat for you to drool over.

■

The urinal's diaphragm approaches the crux
evasively, like Bon Ami

trashing the sink it pretends to clean.
Death to arrangements, says the urinal.

■

This aporia's
hair curls under, a New Look urinal,

a class act, a Clausewitz.
Any moment now the urinal will stage its own funeral.

■

The urinal's deathbed is clogged
with party invitations. Every urinal

contains this information, recycles it,
sends it back to the originating stream.

STREISAND SINGS STRAVINSKY

singled out for transcendence
or hypochondriasis in the rain
I saw rare Barbra LPs for sale

∎

Streisand Sings Stravinsky
Streisand Sings Schoenberg
Streisand Sings Chomsky

∎

cover art: she posed in Cindy
Sherman guise—jaw segments
replaced by rubber and cardboard

∎

lukewarm about my lip's infected lump
Barbra drove a Jaguar
as token of fealty and aphasia

■

I spit blood under her disapproving aegis
and to steal hegemony said I envied
dead Guy Hocquenghem's Elliott Gould curls

■

she ridiculed mock-turtlenecks and warned
"you can catch chronic fatigue syndrome
from pressure cookers and Crock-Pots"

■

to squelch mental gyrations
on a damask fauteuil I accepted extreme unction
while lipsynching a samizdat *Streisand Sings Schiele*

AT THE GRAVE OF

YVONNE DE CARLO

Here is a simple recipe
for moral turpitude with hard sauce.
Yvonne De Carlo died.

I frenched a father's finger.
His omission became my mission.
My luxurious attic life:

a girl ruined or owned it,
nabbed me, sat on me.
I'd misjudged clout levels.

The United States should be washed and folded
and put in its drawer like a good miscreant.
I demand exactitude.

I PROMISED CONNIE FRANCIS

After the epidural
again at the grave
I promised Connie Francis
an actor who used to be handsome.

I promised Connie Francis
his death according to
his death according to the town
his death according to the town crier.

Hypomanic at the Alhambra
I promised Connie Francis
his miniature shameknob.
Listening to K-Y

I promised Connie Francis
to book a facial
on Lillian Gish's birthday*
which turns me on

again at the grave.
More baby food
I promised Connie Francis
according to the town crier.

* Lillian Gish suddenly occurs to me
  as paragon of vulnerable
  beauty and literariness.

ESTATE SALE

On iGavel I bought
a blue glass medallion
once owned by Anna Moffo.

Blue glass medallion:
boys go mad. I dreamt
of a student suddenly alive

again, available, acolyte
material, his name
difficult to spell, an "m"

where I didn't expect it.
Words: collapse, incompetent,
non-coping. More

words: stains, buttons,
objects, littleness, holes,
polyps, aftermaths. All

are sticky. I like this dais.
My desk drawer holds a cache
of father photos—sprocketed

edges. He's "famous"—
no wonder, like a V.P., I
wear white shirt, string tie.

AT THE GRAVE OF RENATA TEBALDI

Recently obtained: photo of Renata in
ermine wrap. Kodak?
Not a treasure. And yet, owning it, I
accept ambiguity: impossible to
train my eye directly on
amaranth.

"Tendentious," a prof once called my Wordsworth
essay. "The reader isn't a potato."
Banished, Renata's voice
(according to me)
lacks emotion, but perhaps I've
dried out, affectively, and need to divorce
"I" from "Thou," or take "Thou" for one last test drive.

DOSSIER OF IRRETRIEVABLES

Last night at Bar 6
I asked an Icelandic superstar

how to say "I have always depended on the kindness
of strangers" in Icelandic and she told me how.

■

My father forewarned me
about Simone Weil's club foot.

In a green Chevy—
the only possible tabernacle

for communicating facts
of deprivation and disease—

he insisted: be nice to Simone,
play with Simone.

An envy molecule,
she will save you from time's encroachment.

■

Unfortunately, in a failed
screen test for *Rebecca*,

Vivien Leigh wore no makeup and revealed
melancholy ordinariness—

uncast Mrs. de Winter,
vulnerable on Waterloo Bridge.

■

Dr. Schreber's butt slid away
or offered hairy contiguity.

Dr. Schreber's butt entered
my house as death ambassador

offering AIDS brotherliness
as surveillance lollipop

to snobs (*c'est moi*)
with rhinestone glasses and Kabuki maquillage.

■

I am a flat, pink, tongued,
funereal flower

associated with a fried chicken restaurant.
I am the palsied boy who annexes the entire yard,

his identity uncertain—troublemaker,
gardener, narcoleptic, dentist?

■

Hush . . . Hush, Sweet Colonoscopy
Hush . . . Hush, Sweet Spam

Hush . . . Hush, Sweet Careerist
Hush . . . Hush, Sweet Untimely Death

■

I dreamt about my typewriter
from Beethoven's point of view—

a fat man or a man
becoming heavy, wading in bloomers,

his unquestionable testicles a cloud
of implication near seaweed.

Fingering my hole, he became
a suicidal crêche

at high noon, no mother in sight—
merely schmutz on a mono *Missa Solemnis*.

THE BITTER TEARS OF

ALEXANDER SCRIABIN

A novel begins here
but I'm too tired to write it.

I caught a computer virus
while googling "James Caan nude."

His hairy chest—*Lady in a Cage*—interrupts
Olivia de Havilland's neurasthenic woundedness.

Scriabin, pugilistic and naïve,
tastes briny. A bird

shat on my head as I crossed Ninth Avenue.
Don't be so inhibited! My bedspread

in Baltimore was a tablecloth
in a long-ago story no one liked, though I polished

its language. At a funeral
I met my great-uncle Melville,

an arbitrageur, a forbidden planet
no astronomer can find. Petrarchan

means the impossible predicament
of a male lover addressing the precipice

while veiling his voice's
aperture. Hair patterns

of porn stars are too stylized. No
topiary, please! Transpose me, klepto shaman.

SPEED BUMPS

My father received a "Best Fake Policeman" prize.
I watched his shtetl ordination through smudged progressives.

When the dermatologist said, "Let me look
under your scrotum," I got semi-hard.

Adrienne Rich entered my dream for a quick visit.
Swarthy, she brought a bag of pretzels to bed.

Evel Knievel—as title and concept—depressed me
until I began to insist on a daily orgasm.

Havelock Ellis urinated on H.D.—
his psychiatric patient. Some details in poems

are factual.
Don't demonize! Later I cut

open my arm and bumped into a former fuck whose new
pectoral tatoo commemorates his dead sister.

FOUR WEIRD WORDS

Schönberg means beautiful mountain.
My last name means tasty tree.

Vanessa Redgrave's saliva: I see it in air.
Chiasmus: X and Y trade places.

Four weird words occur in *Maldoror:*
peccary, rhinolophus, crevasses, elytra.

My house smells of ham hock.
Trapezoidal reflections. Anna Moffo's blue

glass medallion (now mine) receives unseasonable light.
How can you tell if a sniffle is hysteria?

Mother or father: who owned the master bathroom?
Isthmus stains on my cup suggest Magellan's ambitions.

This windowpane has trichinosis:
pucker marks, rain runnels.

LAP DISSOLVE

Kant describes national characteristics
as if he weren't a midget cripple:

blacks this, Persians that.
He mentions a French trait, *indifferentism.*

Retrovir, please. Will insurance cover it?
Dreading action, insistently I hold will

in abeyance. *Pharmakos:* scapegoat
chosen in atonement for crime,

misfortune. Angel unfixes electrodes
attached to my right shoulder.

Seeking his pheromones, I inhale.
In *Mr. Blandings Builds His Dream House,*

Lex Barker impersonates a carpenter
meeting Cary Grant, whose alibi is surprise.

ARCHAIC AWE

My name is Bossyboots.
Liza Minnelli chose me for audience

participation guinea
pig. On a pad

I doodled
Fallopian detours. Later

Liza escaped on a daisy-
festooned tangerine

bike, handlebars
shrink-wrapped, while eating a water biscuit.

SALTINE POEM

On a saltine
I wrote a poem:

salt grains served
as commas, periods.

My grandmother poured
syrup on the saltine,

wept. Her talc
was excessive,

an odor I recognized
in the dark. I seemed

ancient, didactic.
(This part is true.)

She ate my saltine,
minus its nightingale.

WALTER BENJAMIN'S DAD

"And if Dad founded a great literature among them,
Dad did so with face averted.

Dad's universality knew no bounds.
By nature, Dad was not adaptable.

Dad never lost his powerful
dislike of living in big towns.

Conversations with Dad is moreover
one of the finest prose works of the nineteenth century.

Things themselves do not speak but, as it were,
seek Dad's permission to speak."

NATIONAL NUDIST

CLUB NEWSLETTER

Into the unisex nursery's toilet my undershirt falls.
I fish it out and find my face on a marquee.

Florida: in sneakers, I construct
Delft shelves to store scrawled diagnoses.

I enter an observation tank
(rightly considered tragic, irreversible)

to greet the hatchetfaced magician whose dead mother
says *welcome back*, implying I've been fired.

Through Skinner Box glass
he watches me play with dildos, blades. Entranced

by unending orgasm, I dismiss his tendency
to find amelioration in experience's fluctuating shallows.

THE BOOK OF SCAPEGOATS

Click the grief castanets.
Spin your heinie while clacking.

Win a fortune if you clink correctly.
Scald the universe with your castanets.

■

Grandmother pressed her groin
into my thigh. I reciprocated.

She said homosexuality
was a no-no. Otherwise tolerant

she amused herself with Aeschylus
near an orchard's admonishment.

■

If only the pimple had a proper home!
It survives on handouts.

"This isn't true," thinks the pimple,
stepping out for delicatessen.

Will the pimple please explain
its scrunched gait, its grandiosity problem,

its lumière nature
amenable to remembering nickelodeons aglow?

■

At brunch her brass
or copper penis

pops out.
Can't grab it.

Her penis appears
as addendum,

a groove
inside the diatribe.

Not hobbled, she divides
coffee cake into equal pieces.

NO, MY TALK IS NOT ABOUT

HANNAH ARENDT

The guilt-tripper and I
hug near the strip parlor—

his beard black, retributive.
He drinks my bleach.

Afterward, the turnstile.
His unseeing eyes evade, divert, provide.

I need the noun *containment*.
Direct quotation.

■

Off to service a new marine.
The regime of "thirty things":

do thirty things in a row,
each small and purposeful.

I get it: copula
is the root of copulation.

Gros Manseng, Petit Manseng:
eccentric grapes. Gripes.

■

My snack-sized pudding cup
expresses repentance.

The sound of its lid opening
is unfriendly, cosmopolitan.

Pudding sees itself
as brazen. I perceive it

as possessing the odorless, refined
atmosphere of a eunuch evangelist.

■

In 76-degree water
Alban Berg watched Liza Minnelli

gently shred goat into oblivion:
"I noticed she was beautiful &

wanted to call on someone
else to acknowledge that she

was in no ordinary way
extra-incandescent."

SHORT SUBJECTS

Greetings, stomach.
Greetings, humanity.
The girl with foamy hair
walks past a private fountain.

Mother lives on the highest ledge
of the shared bathroom,
her hair dyed blonde
for the masturbator's wedding—

a vegetarian ceremony, Irish.
First there will be a short subject,
then *Those Magnificent Men in Their Flying Machines.*
Find four seats together.

That will be difficult or easy,
depending on the cineplex.
Find a place *not* near fascists
and *not* in the first row.

■

Ash Wednesday, the movie, is
almost as good as *Ash Wednesday*,
the movie. Trumpery. Brisket
confuses patrons who expect

a matinee of *Hair*, haiku-for-hire,
a sneak preview of *Chinatown*
without objectification,
a shot of testosterone as chaser.

■

Greetings, reporters. I bought
a fountain pen to celebrate
The Anna Moffo Timbre Hour.
I'll devote one hour each day

to remembering her timbre,
reactiving its sheen
via my deeds. Welcome
to The Anna Moffo Timbre Hour,

sponsored by Rexall. Recently
I decided to be factual.
Rhetoric travels quickly,
oatmeal-colored against the bulkwark dawn.

FAUVIST DEPRAVITY

O glove compartment,
behold the hollowness
of being promised seventy thousand
identically erotic winding sheets.

Call me torpedo boat
or mons veneris.
Only the globe thistle and the roach clip understand

I used to be your rat-voiced
brother, your drub.

The Hegelian pony, our family
carnival's sure-fire draw,

fails to amend
the gray-shelled turtle's melismatic gloom.

THE ASS FESTIVAL

Pink cum dribbles out my anus.
Nietzsche calls it "The Ass Festival."
The lion roars.

Scientists agree.
I switch to Sanskrit.
Everything happens twice.

We stop being interested.
Like a knee.
I enjoy reading philosophy.

Without a penis.
I understand metaphysics.
Vietnam shapes it.

We live in a totalitarian society.
I'm noun-poor.
The more castrated, the more

optimistic: ratio.

I cum five times in a row.

I ignore denominational details.

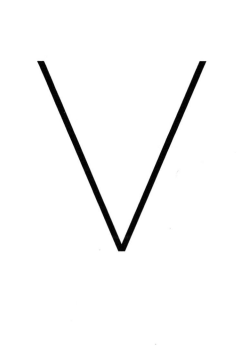

THE ICE CREAM MAN

the ice cream man cometh in my mouth
in my neo-realist playlet the ice cream man
cometh in my Festspielhaus
in my axial plan for the resurrection of Araby

Keith Haring said
the ice cream man cometh for $2,000 plus expenses
in a town car named Jerusalem
cruising on *nachträglichkeit*

dispersing genital catarrh on Karl-Marx-Allee
according to Little Hans directing *Otello*
after Carol Channing the ice cream man cometh
censorship stopped his further progress

the ice cream man cometh bringing news of botulism
bringing full viral load
bringing amputation the ice cream man
singing *A Farewell to Arms*

cometh and Zweig knew the consequences
Kleist predicted the Haiti earthquake
as a pseudonym
the ice cream man cometh cloacally

as a Clotilde pudding in Norma's mouth
the ice cream man cometh with a passport stamped "Desirée"
to my father's house in Knoxville the ice cream man
cometh lexical foam

Don Giovanni's stone guest said
the ice cream man cometh along well said the plastic surgeon
and the Lord opened a KFC franchise
and died of worms or wrath

anagnorisis in his mouth
Tobias Schneebaum the proud cannibal said
the ice cream man cometh for interminable *sesshin*
split-screen the ice cream man to comfort Clara Schumann

cometh into his own as extortionist
seeking *epoché*
derailing the diorama with Theban patience
with Hecuba's permission

the ice cream man cometh yet goeth as Vera Miles in
    Autumn Leaves
with trained diction the ice cream man
fearing dark alleyways and yew
rebutting the cabaletta on borrowed wings cometh

in a poetry book called *The Superhairy*
carpeted in discombobulation
the ice cream man cometh for the Marschallin's levee
in Hofmannsthal's bed to avenge Rosa Luxemburg

to found the Mattachine
for Passover the ice cream man
cometh as atheism's finest flower slain
on language's birthday

prematurely the ice cream man cometh as Coffy
a lyric drama for harmonica
the ice cream man cometh to sip Mnemosyne juice
spitting stichomythia the ice cream man

cometh to catch crabs from Heinrich Heine
in the guise of Peggy Guggenheim's fifth dog
the ice cream man cometh in from the cold
as plagiarist on a bender the ice cream man without qualities
    cometh

to eat Medicaid for breakfast
as swing vote the ice cream man cometh
according to Al Capone and John le Carré
against the best wishes of Merrill Moore the forgotten sonneteer

to Warsaw the ice cream man
cometh to dial BUtterfield 8
to dispute Truman Capote's greatness
to correspond with Madame de Sevigné's other daughter the
    ice cream man

as prison chaplain and cantor
cometh to trash JFK's Brookline birthplace
reincarnated as Schopenhauer the ice cream man
cometh to urinate on the fire

fouling my website
lamenting dukkha the ice cream man cometh
go fetch the dead baby said Kostelnička
to ordinate my father and Genet's saltimbanque lover the ice
    cream man

cometh as Cher's revenge
revamping Darwin
inadequately and after long delay
unlike Godot the ice cream man

cometh unlike Todd-AO
as we sank into the arms of Daniel Boone
with no help from Walt Disney
the ice cream man unaware of Heisenberg

cometh to give pop quizzes on theories of time
sans RSVP the ice cream man cometh
in dreams begin anal responsiveness
singing sick lieder

the ice cream man in a Ginger Rogers sweater set
cometh dramaturging *Götterdämmerung*
to correct lapses in taste and efface confessions
as Edna St. Vincent Millay woke up

the unavenged ambitions of the Hiroshima maidens
the bump and grind of the Rhine maidens
shedding housewife psychosis
as Marie Corelli predicted

over Bertha Pappenheim's dead body
conspicuously consuming Veblen's Taj
Martha Bernays cometh and Sigismund too
the scrutinized synagogue cometh

the tribadites cometh quarantined
the infantile masturbators cometh
to afterlife's after-party
the ice cream man to Gautama's tree

in every flavor cometh not attached to grandiose location
as Artaud foresaw in asylum
the ice cream man cometh to heal hemorrhagic stroke
in 1963 bearing missiles and Fudgsicles

Glenn Gould cometh Merv Griffin cometh dogmatically
pursuing the Brothers Grimm with swich licour
according to Christina Rossetti's goblin sisters
to exercise the human capacity for concentration

libido in German is *libido*
the ice cream man cometh speaking ruin
where pause becomes timorous
in pillar of fire obscure

incrementally the ice cream man cometh grasping totem
the demand for clarity unsated
without commentary the ice cream man cometh undone
over time
as time interrupts its own egress

INCREMENTS

Spending one minute
listening to cars
on Tenth Avenue
isn't criminal.

Today I tipped
the hair stylist
five dollars.
Last time, I tipped

ten. Attenuation
means thinness
but also in-
tensification?

New stylistic
mandate: imitate
my fourth-grade
diary. Avoid

if-then clauses.
Circumvent
laudanum's
lure. That's an

if-then clause
in hiding. At
Hotel Arcobaleno
a cockroach colonized

my zitti. Dreamt
I bought a Nazi
coloring book
for a kid I'd liberated.

Dreamt a dental
hygienist said
my mouth was
yellow and green.

My low-bosomed
great-aunt in 1952
had a hysterectomy
immediately before

my parent's wedding.
Guilt: I bought Dior
Homme silver
sneakers. Recent

deaths: Leon Kirchner, 90.
Claude Lévi-Strauss, 100.
Dairy relief pills smell
appalling, like lamb.

Dreamt Alejandro Rey
(hiding from cyclones)
in *The Flying Nun*
visited D. H. Lawrence's

slum home and demanded
a lube job. Removing
hiphuggers, I succumbed
to terminal graphomania.

Prince of increments,
I saw, in a pool's far
lane, the Semitic cutie
who shaves his tubby

body. His schnitzel
sagged, near Bosc pears
and turnips, severed
from abundant greens.

Why morbidly
punctuate? My Portuguese
lemon, not tart, tastes
like Play-Doh's unsung

fount. Play-Doh Factory,
I loved your poop
ambience, extruded quadri-
laterals vast yet squat.

APRIL IN VENICE

With copper hair and five
o'clock shadow and odd
glasses I look Italian.

Better make sure my face
doesn't get fat.
Water sends jaundiced

light onto buildings.
Bridges appear
asymmetrical, as do

church facades: angles
and perspectival biases,
illusions. Deserted

Dorsoduro. Waiter with
shaved head and eyes
sometimes shifty sometimes

direct. Can we trust Tiepolo's
mimetic space, or is he
shitting us? Organic oranges:

I nearly wrote "origin."
Palsied young kid in stroller,
lion incongruous on pillar,

lollipops of Doge's Palace,
different colored marbles like
souk not organized into coherent

religious experience. Overcast.
Stooped woman's vehement
drag of cig. Catty-corner

house's blue and white
laundry. No linen hung out
in public is spectacular.

Can't figure out how to play
phone messages on lodging's
machine. Continue no matter

what is always the solution.
Artist never rewarded
for work that sustains

future world is point
of David Markson's
This Is Not a Novel.

"Mulino Stucky,"
phrase repeated because fun,
sticky, mulish. Emptied

(pacified) intestines.
Not enough said in
redundant homage

to San Marco. Overall
impression: Virgin Mary
always wears same Moorish outfit.

Listening to Poulenc
two-piano sonata though
it's not Venetian.

Two men with tardive
dyskinesia in bacaro
where we killed

an hour before dinner.
Assignment: make
book of Conté crayon

studies, one color per
page, fifty monochrome
"works on paper."

Why not write as if translating
every word, English a difficult
yearned-for commodity?

Some critics say Poulenc had
attention deficit disorder—
at least his melodies did.

I own two pianos
but only one language,
and *I don't own it* is

premise of this plodding
investigation. We shall
continue with utmost formality

toward absent destination.
Yesterday, my father's birthday,
also, first day of Passover—

I mentioned Passover but not
birthday in postcard to him.
Water pressure uneven: cold and hot

cycle according to system
we'll never learn. *Sorry, I don't use*

frequently your language.
Straight men showing off
include me accidentally

in their bacchanal. Nostalgic
sudsy fruit-candy
smell may be SVELTO soap

or my synesthetic
response to Poulenc sextet.
Waiter described almond

eyes as characteristically Venetian.
We already "belong"—
trannie who works desk

at gym said "ciao"
when seeing us near
Campo Santa Margarita.

Dogs rutting beside
table: small male pooch
licked big female's

interested genitals.
Synagogue: kippahs
are comfortable,

mine bright blue.
My lightly sacrilegious
treatise, still

embryonic: *A Jew*
Looks at the Virgin Mary.
Write poems ecstatically

apprehending the obvious
in Hagiwara Sakutarō's style
or one-line poems with

such titles as "Malice
Aforethought" or "Evening
Amid Primroses."

Dreamt Liz's inbetweenness
flustered and infuriated its possessor,
like a violin gripped too tightly.

Laundry in Venice,
beneath green shutters you thrive,
learn stiffness by evening.

Tomorrow, visit Lido
cemetery, Jews
since 1300 interred, islanded.

_____ (proper name)
has five syllables
and that is my poem

was a poem I wrote, aloud,
upon entering Campiello San
Lorenzo at 9 or so tonight

in light rain but now I
can't remember the magical five-
syllable name that made those

three lines a poem.
Often the Virgin Mary
looks lazy, waiting,

between tasks—or is she
stunned by hormones,
family pressures, lethargic

attention to death's grimace?
Green light refracted
off canals onto green shutters

repeats without reservation.
Melon has serial number
tattooed on its bark.

In peacock hat I feel
anonymous, strange, not easily
categorized. Some bridges

are steeper and face
unpredicted directions.
Each church is merely

a church, reduced
or exalted to its age-
old office and circumstance.

Half the time I'm not fully
present to spectacle
of *consciousness*, a word

I've avoided for years—
my father's property.
Exhausted. Boat to Burano,

city of colored exact
small houses brightly
caparisoned. Unabashedly

I touched (with Jew
hand) Pound's grave.
Are this album's Benares

singers bewailing
the absence of honey?
Today in mirror

my face seems wide,
a fact I can't
reconcile with long

jaw, high forehead,
large nose, narrow
eyes—insufficient

difference between pupil
and iris. Someone in
window unverifiable

distance from mine
slowly lowers shade.
Burano man stepped

carelessly on live
crab he'd caught. Startled
I said "Ow!" and winced—

perpetrator didn't blink.
I wanted to tell lace vendor
"Your perfume smells good"

in Italian but feared
I'd mistakenly say
"You stink." Life

half over. Don't mind dying,
signing off. *Sono*
stupido I said at dinner.

Dream: told Mia Farrow
that whenever I visited
the Dakota I recalled

Rosemary's Baby and hoped
she didn't resent being
permanently Polanski.

Gesuati's twisty
altar: maybe today
I'll desecrate holy water fonts.

Twenty years of galley slavery
for getting baptised four times:
medieval Jew wanted conversion's

perks repeatedly. Jews
remain news. I dipped
fingers in San Nicolò da

Tolentino's holy water
and pretended to cross
myself—sudden desire

for damp fingers. Subversive
inconsequence of San
Marco's snoozing lion.

Doge's Palace never budges.
Anachronistic, it establishes
perimeters but lacks

bossiness. Bridge
of Sighs, sinister
Band-Aid connecting

judgment and detention.
How many times need
church bells ring to convince

astounded populace
it's 7:30?
Few evidently

gay people here.
Literati, glitterati, eviscerati.
Moon, still sickle. I spend

peripheral mental
energy staring at
ground expecting

dog shit. Dream:
in Nazi Germany
I proclaimed obsessive fondness

for Goethe, thereby
laying claim to life-
saving Germanness.

My sister proclaimed
fondness for Goethe's
sister, didn't understand

only allegiance to Goethe
himself would pass
muster with Hitler's spies.

Did I pretend attachment
to Goethe's works
or to a character named "Goethe"

who sometimes appeared
in Goethe's writings?
Dream: kitten crossing

sidestreet off Madison
was grazed by car
and officially "traumatized."

Cat's obligation (prior
to injury) was carrying
ten books, but traumatized

cat couldn't continue
lifting literature.
Now hands reach

out window to gather
aforementioned laundry.
We said goodbye

to loyal *fruttivendolo*
couple: *"Domani,*
ritornerò alla patria

mia." La prossima
volta is a useful phrase.
Tell me how to use it.

ACKNOWLEDGMENTS

The author thanks the editors of the following publications, in which these poems, sometimes in different versions, previously appeared:

The Awl: "Archaic Awe," "The Bitter Tears of Alexander Scriabin," "Dossier of Irretrievables"

A Best of FENCE: The First 9 Years, Volume I: "Investigation"

Black Clock: "Urinals," "Faust's Dog"

Black Warrior Review: "Good Morning, Marienbad," "Grooming in America"

Boulevard Magenta: "Poem on Pink Construction Paper," "Hot Scenes with Undead Hematologists"

Canarium 1: "Nebbish Archive," "I Promised Connie Francis," "Saturnalia," "Four Weird Words," "Lap Dissolve"

Divining Divas, ed. Michael Montlack (Lethe Press, 2012): "Estate Sale"

EOAGH: "The Tidbit School of Adult Entertainment," "Pointillism," "No, My Talk Is Not About Hannah Arendt"

Electronic Poetry Review: "At the Grave of Yvonne De Carlo," "National Nudist Club Newsletter"

Fence: "Fauvist Depravity," "Investigation"

Hanging Loose: "April in Venice"

The Hat: "Possessiveness," "Crawl Spaces," "At the Grave of Renata Tebaldi"

Jacket: "Short Subjects"

LIT: "Accretion," "Return of the Noun"

Opium: "At the Grave of Fernando Pessoa"

Portable Boog Reader #4: "Saltine Poem"

Queer Voice, ed. Ingrid Schaffner (Institute of Contemporary Art, Philadelphia, 2010): "Streisand Sings Stravinsky"

Shampoo: "The Book of Scapegoats," "Little Ode to Incorrigibility," "Estate Sale," "The Ass Festival"

Under the Rock Umbrella: Contemporary American Poets from 1951–1977, ed. William Walsh (Mercer University Press, 2006): "At the Grave of Renata Tebaldi"

Women's Studies Quarterly: "The New Brutalism"